NLP

There Is A Book On Neuro-Linguistic Programming That Has Powerful Techniques For Mind-taking, You Will Be Able To Dominate The People You Speak With With The Help Of This Book

(How It Enhances Concentration And Provides Better Control Of Emotions)

Elbrus Borisov

TABLE OF CONTENT

What Is NLP ? 1

Who Uses Dark Psychology? 13

Learning Techniques To Improve One's Ability To Learn 23

Exposed: NLP Metamodel Sales Applications! 26

NLP : What Is It? Hypnotic Language Patterns: What Are They? 43

Prioritizing The Most Important Matters 58

Mind Control Techniques 66

NLP 's Ethical Applications 76

Rethink Patterns To Direct People's Thoughts In The Way You Desire 83

What Does The Dark Triad Aspect Look Like In People? 96

Enhancing Academic Performance 134

NLP Techniques And Strategies For Everyday Life 149

The Essentials Of Reading People 164

What Is NLP ?

Understanding the acronym NLP , its complete meaning, applications, advantages, and disadvantages is necessary to grasp the subject matter easily and clearly. The term Neuro-Linguistic Programming is represented by the acronym NLP . It also consists of three distinct parts.

To put it simply, there are three components to Neuro-Linguistic Programming:

Neuro: This refers to the nervous system.

Linguistic: The language that's being utilized

Programming: This is the term for the neural function language.

Neuro-Linguistic Programming, to put it briefly, is the language of the mind. An easy example will clarify things for us. Have you ever found it difficult to comprehend someone when communicating with them? A language barrier can be one of the causes. This primarily occurs when you are from a different area.

This is what happens when you travel to a new nation, feel hungry, and choose to search for a restaurant. You are disappointed when you see lamb chops on the menu since you had planned to order a steak. This results from the normal interaction between an individual and their unconscious mind. All people desire a happy life, a better relationship, harmony with family members, physical well-being, a balanced diet, and financial abundance. However, the final result may irritate when there is inadequate expectation delivery and improper communication.

NLP strongly claims that the conscious mind is always the goal-setter and the unconscious mind is unquestionably the goal-getter. Simply put, nobody's unconscious mind exists to frustrate or discourage others. However, its purpose is to assist you in accomplishing your goals and fulfilling your mission. The negative aspects arise from improper communication, high expectations, and a lack of a clearly defined goal. More "Lamp Chops" will soon be served, and there will be a persistent sense of frustration.

Currently, a broad understanding of what NLP is exists. We now need to understand NLP's technical justification and application. To put it simply, NLP is about striking a balance between communication and personal growth. The three elements—the linguistic, neuro-neuro, and behavioral patterns that an individual possesses and has learned throughout experiences—were related to one another. They also thought there was a chance the elements may be changed to help someone fulfilltheir objectives and realize their ambitions.

Grinder and Bandler contend that anyone can acquire the skills necessary to become extraordinary and that NLP techniques can help people hone their abilities. Additionally, they claim that NLP techniques can be used to cure a variety of illnesses, including learning problems, allergies, tic disorders, melancholy, phobias, and shortsight.

When they provide seminars, workshops, or training sessions for individual enterprises or government organizations, most firms and hypnotists utilize nonverbal language processing (NLP) for marketing purposes. NLP is not a pseudoscience, and no proof supports the assertions made. It is considered outdated and unable to provide precise information about the brain's functioning. There are claims that the theory underlying the neurological approach is flawed.

It is claimed that the claims made by Bandler and Grindr are unsupported by any evidence and have weaknesses in the technique. It is thought that more than two investigations have yielded more compelling results than the ones that Bandler, Grinder, and even other practitioners deemed extraordinary. Several hypnotherapists have embraced this technique. Even enterprises that provide marketing and training services to corporations and government organizations.

The Effects of the Mind, Both Conscious and Unconscious

Has it ever occurred to you to alter just one personal habit? You are going to give up one habit. One such habit could be: • Is it feasible to give a presentation without getting tense or nervous?

Minimize the amount of time spent on social media in minutes and hours; Prevent procrastination by completing tasks on time; and Limit the number of snacks you eat at once, such as a bowl of ice cream or crackers.

The Mind's Two Consciousnesses

Once that's accomplished, you can accomplish your objectives. This is because your subconscious mind constantly believes you need that. Since the brain typically employs NLP as a manual, accepting its use is akin to teaching your mind. Until you've trained it to speak fluently in your language, your unconscious mind will recognize what you need and think it's crucial for your survival, making it function like a helpful "server."

Excellent interpersonal and group communication is another aspect of NLP .Mostly created using methods and models that are regarded as superior and effective.Primarily employed by therapists who see outcomes with their patients. Most people think NLP is just a collection of methods, strategies, and resources. However, it goes beyond that; it also refers to the mindset and strategies employed to recognize the intended objectives and the means of achieving favorable outcomes. Understanding the techniques and strategies employed is crucial for managing one's mental health, emotional state, and life.

The Background of NLP

After learning about the significance and application of NLP , it's critical to understand its origins. It is well known that Brandler and Grinler, the pioneers of this theory, described NLP as a collection of plans, the approach taken from the outset of implementation. They took the concept from various sources, including Virginia Satir, Fritz Peris, and Milton Erickson. They also drew on the theories of Alfred Korzybski, Gregory Bateson, and Noam Chomsky. And combined that with Carlos Castaneda's strategies, plans, tactics, and concepts.

They wrote their 1975 book intending to use it for therapeutic approaches. They assert the approach will seamlessly integrate with their therapeutic framework to promote healing. They explained that the purpose of their method is to assist in gathering data to question a client's language and stimulate their thought process. And that there is a very high likelihood of recovery when the language component is questioned, and general information is provided.

Since NLP first emerged many years ago, the technique and approach have developed significantly, and it is now used for a wide range of problems and circumstances. The core concepts of NLP are behavior, habits, and observation. And identifying and disclosing the living patterns that will function effectively is the aim. Additionally, be aware of the patterns that are not effective. It is advisable to reinforce what works and identify and alter what doesn't work once the patterns are known.

Who Uses Dark Psychology?

A lot of people will take advantage of dark psychology. We frequently assume this is an uncommon occurrence rather than something common or necessary. And since we believe we will be able to identify it long before it affects our lives, we like to take pride in our ability to remain as far away as possible. In light of the concepts discussed in the preceding chapter, it is reasonable to conclude that anyone can use dark psychology to influence others to achieve their goals. If they're not too far gone, anyone might harm the target to obtain what they need or accomplish their objectives. Most of us will presume that we never feel at ease hurting those around us. For most people, the fear of experiencing regret and shame during the process is a sufficient disincentive to use dark psychology and some of the other methods we will cover in this article. There is still a certain amount of dark psychology within us. A few will maintain it somewhat louder than the others. Certain people can control their impulses to reject thoughts and activities they may feel compelled to conduct. We will not injure people and withstand the laws, ethics, and other obstacles preventing us from working on this. After that, certain people will experience these urges but are generally able to manage them. They don't necessarily go for targets to upset someone else. However, there can come a moment when they hurt someone else, or maybe they see someone else getting hurt and have no regrets. In the process, they may feel slightly pleased with themselves, particularly if this has enabled them to achieve their goals. Most of the time, they can still control these evil impulses. There will also be people who cannot control these negative urges or lack the will or means to try eliminating them. They may believe people are foolish if they do not attempt to use them to achieve their goals. If something or someone helps them achieve their goals, they have no difficulty using it. Trying to acquire what they want from them often hurts someone else. These manipulators can have other objectives in mind. They could make every effort to accomplish their objective. Using someone if they are not hurt in the process is okay. The dark manipulator won't feel guilty if someone has to harm themselves to accomplish their objectives. This implies that they are liable for any injury caused to another individual, even if it is not their intention to do so. You'll also discover that many people will fit into these categories; however, this does not imply that they work in one industry or another. They may have numerous friends or none and come from any social or economic background. It is hard to predict who will be in dark psychology and who will be able to control some of their urges because there isn't always a set of people who are more inclined to lean one way or the other. All the same, you should be happy with this. It implies that regardless of your origins or history, you can apply dark psychology. Some of the most skilled and cunning manipulators in the world weren't prepared for this level of success, or at least that wasn't what others assumed. This enables them to communicate their objectives and join the group of their choice without raising suspicions. We possess dark psychology, but most are too afraid to explore it and discover where it takes us. This theory is that sometimes, taking care of yourself and your aims is more important than worrying about other people's intentions or following societal standards. It does not imply that we must go out and cause others as much misery and pain as possible. Here, judging when each circumstance is most justifiable will be essential. To help you be prepared to utilize each dark psychology technique when the time is perfect, this guide will walk you through a few alternative approaches. We've talked for a while about how, at some point, we could all employ dark psychology to help us accomplish our objectives and get the outcomes we want. It's time to examine a few demographic groups that are more inclined to employ these strategies and don't hesitate to employ some dark psychology in their social interactions. Nevertheless, You could be shocked at the number of individuals in your life who will take advantage of dark psychology and may have already used you to further their agenda. Those in your life who may benefit from dark psychology include:

1. Narcissists: The self-esteem of those who fit the clinical description of narcissists will be exaggerated. They dream that others will beautify them and need other people around to reinforce their sense of superiority. If necessary, they will resort to coercion, devious

reasoning, unethical reasoning, and other tactics.

2. Sociopaths: Those who are truly sociopathic will be charming, bright, and impulsive. These sociopaths would employ some dubious methods to create a false relationship and help the other person as they lack emotionality and the capacity for regret.

3. Attorneys: Some attorneys will emphasize unusual persuasion techniques and other strategies to get the intended outcome because they are so intent on winning the case.

4. Politicians: These strategies are frequently employed by politicians to persuade the public that they are correct and to win over votes.

5. Sellers: A lot of sellers may act unethically in an attempt to close a deal and will employ dubious methods. Even if they can track their customers, they will use this to persuade and inspire the other person, their customers, to purchase a product.

6. Leaders: Some leaders will employ these dubious methods to get their subordinates to comply, put forth more effort, or perform better.

7. Public Speakers: Knowing that this results in the sale of numerous things in the back of the room and that they can obtain what the audience wants to train, some speakers will be pleased to employ these dubious techniques to raise the audience's emotional state.

8. Anyone Selfish: This includes anyone who prioritizes themselves over others. Even if it means hurting someone else, they will employ this strategy to prioritize their demands. If someone gets hurt in the process, it doesn't matter to them.

Shady tactics guarantee that individuals get what they want regardless of the consequences, even if someone else is harmed. However, there are many other situations in which manipulation and persuasion are safer and more effective ways to achieve your goals.

Learning Techniques To Improve One's Ability To Learn

People can learn more in various ways, increasing their potential for learning. Reading is among the most popular among them, as is engaging in hands-on activities that demand that a person immerse himself fully in the learning process to get firsthand experience. Learning Rx has divided the various learning methods into kinesthetic, visual, and aural categories.

If someone learns best by doing things that need sound, they are considered auditory learners. For instance, many junior high school kids perform exceptionally well on their tests after hearing their professors' discussions. Some study techniques involve recording your professor's talk or your voice summarizing the material you have learned. Some people even memorize poetry by just reading the verses aloud.

Conversely, a person is deemed a visual learner if his primary source of knowledge is what he has seen and experienced. Subjectively, young children are more suited for this type of learning. Kindergartens and some month-old babies typically have access to visual aids that demonstrate basic concepts such as colors, alphabet letters, and other things that kids can learn at a very young age. Some people assert that their memory of it improves after seeing or even watching something.

Here is the third learning style—kinesthetic learning—that some people find more successful than visual learning. This kind of instruction incorporates practical experience. This indicates that after engaging in the real learning process, a person can efficiently gain knowledge. For instance, if a budding chorister didn't sing every note the song called for, they wouldn't develop into good ones. In addition to the previous example, taking notes while a professor reviews mathematical theorems or technical phrases that need to be learned falls under kinesthetic learning.

Considering the three primary learning styles, it is important to remember that every person learns differently and that the speed at which they pick up knowledge varies depending on their learning style. It is important to remember that information acquisition is not limited to those who prefer the previously listed learning styles. These days, NLP is one of the methods that helps people increase their learning rate.

Exposed: NLP Metamodel Sales Applications!

"It's not what you say, it's how you say it" is an old proverb. Salespeople frequently find it difficult to explain their goods and services. Salespeople must know exactly where they are failing in this field, and it is crucial to communicate with a potential customer clearly and compellingly. Understanding NLP Meta Models can help resolve these situations by improving communication. This How-To guide aims to improve a sales professional's ability to close any kind of contract.

NLP Meta Models: Why Are They Important?

The parts of communication, including language-related faults, are represented by NLP Meta Models. Their objective is to minimize the gaps that impede an individual's communication capacity. When salespeople struggle to find the right things to say, they lose the customer's connection. It is crucial to use language correctly if you want the customer to be impressed with the good or service you are offering.

Before you start, you should be aware of: The following tips give a general overview of meta-models and how they are used:

First, unfinished words and phrases that can be made effective are analyzed in meta-model patterns.

Second, maintain your attention. The secret is to communicate clearly and intelligibly with the least amount of distortion possible.

Finally, remember that making needless changes to well-constructed sentences can lead to misunderstandings.

The different Meta-Model Patterns: In this section, we'll discuss the most prevalent meta-model patterns that influence how well a salesperson can persuade a potential client.

Broad generalizations: These are mistakes that ignore exclusions. Sellers may generalize remarks to illustrate a point, painting an incorrect picture by failing to clarify any potential "ifs" or "buts." Full disclosure is required in this case.

Generalizations that confine descriptions to one extreme are known as universal quantifiers. When additional terms like "some," "many," and "most" are used, the truth value is reduced when the terms "every" or "none" are used.

Lost Performatives: These phrases may convey an air of authority and can have an unpleasant implication. For instance, "This product will make your life much easier" suggests the customer has a challenging life. So, to prevent negativity, their utilization should be restricted.

Modal Operators: When the term "must" is used needlessly, it can hurt a transaction since it gives the impression that the buyer is being pushed to make a decision and that it is more of a choice than an order.

Eliminations: One problem with omissions is that they leave out important details that the vendor sincerely attempts to convey, making the information ambiguous or unhelpful. His potential attempt at manipulation by withholding information is a further cause for concern. The vendor has to proceed cautiously to prevent this.

Absence of Referential Index: When the term "they" is used imprecisely without identifying the precise parties involved, mistrust may result.

Vendors ought to strive for diversity since mentioning powerful figures can enhance the reputation of the good or service. The act of using the pronoun "they" diminishes the credibility of a fact. adding "People love this product" is not as effective as adding "Your neighbor, Mr. X, placed three orders yesterday!" Naturally, only if it's accurate!

Comparative Deletions: A statement ends abruptly and becomes meaningless without further comparison. There must be a second good or service that is being compared if phrases like "better than," "superior to," or "more useful than" are being utilized.

Distortions: Exaggerations that occasionally distort the argument a seller is attempting to make are known as distortions. Since its usage gives off an air of oddity, it must always be carefully avoided. It is an overstatement to say that "more than half the city's population uses this product" instead of "This product is widely used."

Nominalizations: When it's not necessary, action verbs can be changed from verbs of action to nouns to add additional meanings. It may potentially lead to communication breakdowns and further complicate matters.

Mind Reading: When vendors assert that they can read their customers' thoughts, it can be bothersome to adopt the 'I know what you are thinking' meta-model. Additionally, it can result in humiliating outcomes; thus, it should be avoided.

Reason and Consequence Distortions: Most individuals don't consider the potential causes of a situation; instead, they simply consider its effects. Salespeople must keep an eye out for these patterns and ensure that they have an unbiased understanding of each of these factors.

Assumptions: Assumptions are a type of presupposition. These can harm the sales industry because experts should rely more on data and past experiences rather than making assumptions about potential customer reactions. A poor transaction could arise from drawing incorrect conclusions from presumptions.

The technique of connecting an unconnected cause to an entirely random consequence is known as a complex equivalency. A salesman employing this meta-model pattern without assurance may affect the buyer's perception of reality. For instance, it would be untrue if a salesperson stated that a previous customer bought a property because he bought his lucky ring.

The work of Richard Bandler, a student at the University of California, Santa Cruz, and his instructor, John Grinder, is primarily responsible for the roots of NLP . The sources of inspiration were family therapist Virginia Satir and the late Gestalt therapist Fritz Perls. Later on, they took further inspiration from the works of Alfred Korzybski and Gregory Bateson, especially regarding modeling human thought and behavior. A thorough analysis of Milton H. Erickson, MD's work produced one of the most significant contributions. They referred to it as the Milton model, and Erickson's work helped them see its worth despite its ambiguity and metaphor. Other popular models Grinder, Bandler, and their first pupils created were representational systems, anchoring, reframing, submodalities, and perceptual postures.

Why learn about NLP ?

Modeling and methods are two terms you'll often hear during NLP training. A significant portion of the area concentrates on the capacity to condense human behavior into feasible models and then construct methods based on those models to bring about the desired change.

Models can be viewed as generic theoretical constructions that aid in understanding a class of behavior or as a simplified version of a particular activity, such as the methods employed by a skilled speller or golfer to communicate fear or phobia. Through an awareness of a general model (like the NLP Communications Model, which I will cover in a moment), a clinician can identify problematic expressions quickly and help a patient achieve more understanding and clarity. Furthermore, if a trainer or coach truly comprehends what makes a person function at a high level, they may be able to instill the same caliber of behavior in someone else.

With any luck, this brief overview of the applications of NLP models and methods will help you see the importance of studying this area. As a clinician, I am aware of the opportunities that present themselves when I have a deeper understanding of a patient's mental health and employ a particular approach to provide a successful solution. I can better comprehend optimal performance as a trainer or coach and assist a client in modeling and replicating it. This is essentially where NLP's value lies.

Results that could be seen led to the general acceptance of NLP, which coincided with the human potential movement. As previously mentioned, because these findings were not from academic or scientific institutions and came from a diverse group of practitioners—many of whom had no training in psychology or psychiatry—many institutional stakeholders rejected NLP and are still reluctant to include it in traditional clinical education. However, NLP has always piqued the imagination of many clinicians seeking a quick treatment option.

The Model of NLP Communications

The NLP Communications Model is the one model that, in my opinion, best captures the essence of neuro-linguistic programming. In essence, it aims to elucidate the events that start with outside factors and culminate in distinct and subtle human behavior.

The revelation that we filter our views was a significant contribution. Indeed, we do eliminate some parts of our perception. Our brains automatically and rapidly try to comprehend perceptual input, leading us to generalize—that is, classifying external objects according to similarities or differences. Then, when we attempt to fit our senses into our preconceived or preprogrammed patterns, we frequently misrepresent what we see.

Either consciously or subconsciously, this filtering may take place. As a result, an internal representation is created, resulting from our desire to comprehend. An interior feeling, such as amazement, terror, joy, comfort, etc., is produced by this. Thus, our physiology expresses this in turn. A state's physiological expression could be as evident as a shift in expression or posture. It could even be as minor as a change in peripheral skin temperature, galvanic skin response (GSR), or any other reaction that resembles biofeedback.

Although the concept asserts that a person's condition determines their conduct, this was not fully clarified until Bandler talked about how people strongly desire to hold onto what they know and are accustomed to.

NLP : What Is It? Hypnotic Language Patterns: What Are They?

To better grasp what we're about to study, let's go over the fundamentals before we get started.

The term "Neuro-linguistic Programming," or NLP , refers to the three main pillars upon which human experience is based: language, programming, and neurology. The neurological system regulates the body's numerous systems; language deals with our internal and interpersonal communication; and programming studies models and systems in our environment and how we interpret their inputs to produce desired results. These three fundamental factors are shown by NLP , along with the strong relationship that exists between our mind (Neuro), language (Linguistic), and behavior (Programming).

The foundation of neurolinguistic programming is two fundamental theories:

1.) The zone is not on the map.

I know this may seem confusing at first, but stick with me! According to "The map is not the zone," humans can only ever know what they believe to be a reality, meaning they will never truly know reality. Humans use their senses to react to everything in their environment. There will be differences between the feelings and emotions I get from viewing a certain movie and the ones I get from seeing the same movie. Similarly, two hiking path maps may differ significantly despite depicting the same actual trail. The trail is not the same as the map.

Similarly, rather than reality itself, their neuro-linguistic maps of reality determine a person's conduct and give it meaning. Usually, a person's interpretation of reality is what propels or restrains them rather than reality itself.

2.) The intellect and life are finished processes.

The many interactions that occur between people and their surroundings, as well as within an individual, are structured. The universe, society, and the human body are all subsystems of a larger system that interacts and impacts one another.

The two previously mentioned ideas are combined to create the models and methods that make up the foundation of NLP . According to NLP , it is difficult for people to know the objective truth. It also teaches that as humans cannot make a "true" map of the world, wisdom, ethics, and order cannot be found by possessing one.

Rather, the objective is to produce the most comprehensive map feasible while honoring the structures that oversee the world and ourselves. Those with a map that allows them to see the greatest number of options and viewpoints are the most productive. NLP is about opening your mind to possibilities you never imagined. Multiple options lead to excellence, and insight is gained from various viewpoints.

The NLP founders

Richard Bandler and John Grinder founded neuro-linguistic programming. Their aim in the 1970s was to produce concrete representations of human brilliance. Their first joint work, The Structure of Magic, delineated the actions and speech patterns of two colleagues, Virginia Satir and Fritz Perls. Milton's Patterns of Hypnotic Techniques was released shortly afterward. H. Erickson, who looked into the speech and behavior patterns of one of the most well-known psychiatrists in history, Erickson.

With their separate contributions, Grinder and Bandler codified their methods and discoveries from their early efforts, which they termed "Neuro-linguistic Programming." The intention was to represent the connection between the body, language, and brain.

Over time, NLP has evolved and gained new abilities and instruments for transformation and communication. These days, NLP is very useful in many professional domains, including sales, psychotherapy, creative, law, counseling, education, and more.

Since the field of NLP first emerged in the middle of the 1970s, a great deal has changed, expanded globally, and impacted many lives. A new generation of NLP practitioners emerged in the 1990s, concentrating on problems like vision, mission, and identity.

Patterns of Hypnotic Language

Direct hypnosis and indirect hypnosis are the two types of hypnosis. When most people hear "hypnosis," they typically picture a client or subject sitting with a hypnotherapist. This is known as direct hypnosis. The hypnotist employs many approaches to induce a hypnotic state in the client. The customer will frequently have their eyes closed and appear to be in a comfortable state. Another option is self-hypnosis, in which a person generates a hypnotic state.

We are going to talk about indirect hypnosis today. A collection of words and phrases known as hypnotic language patterns are combined to form a certain sentence structure. This sentence form frequently works without the subject or subjects being aware of it, creating an indirect hypnotic state.

That is why applying Hypnotic Language Patterns is sometimes called "Covert Hypnosis." Once more, this gives off an ominous vibe, as though you're attempting to trick your subjects and make them do something against their will.

Nothing can be false! Thanks to hypnotic language patterns, your subjects will genuinely come to their conclusions. There are two situations: Either utilize hypnotic language patterns, or 1.) make entreaties. The intention is the same in all contexts; hence, it is not malevolent.

It's just that the second choice is a more systematic, well-organized approach.

Now that you know hypnotic language patterns and NLP fundamentals, let's explore some applications!

Identifying Our FavoriteSubmodality

How do we decide which of the different submodalities we prefer? How, moreover, can we approximate what other people's submodalities are? We can make use of two primary procedures: reviewing our communication patterns and historical choices and performance in particular domains.

When every submodality is active, we usually make the finest choices and function at our best, but our performance will decline when our dominant submodality is not active. This may provide a crucial and unmistakable hint about our inclination. For instance, a person sensitive to the visual submodality would find great satisfaction in watching a quiet video with captions. Even when the aural component is absent, the visually focused person is not greatly affected. That individual will probably find it difficult to follow a complex audio recording without a transcript. Performance will suffer if the visual element is removed. On the other hand, because they strongly prefer auditory submodality, they will find it difficult to concentrate when reading because they won't be receiving any auditory input. Determining one's chosen submodality is consequently essential to learning and decision-making since an environment devoid of one's most favoredsubmodality would result in poor information absorption and, eventually, in decisions that are either misinformed or underinformed.

Listening for minute linguistic variations can also discern someone's preferred submodality. Examine the following claims:

"I have a good grasp of what you're saying."

"I see what you mean."

"I hear you loud and clear."

These are all indicators of the speaker's preferred submodality. In the first, kinesthetic is associated; in the second, visual; and in the third, auditory. While we may be able to see ourselves during the day connecting speech or thinking to a specific submodality, this hint is most useful when determining what other people are most sensitive to.

We can also infer someone's preferred submodality by subjectively assessing their interactions. For instance, auditory people tend to talk and move more rhythmically and may exhibit more patterns. They may be highly talkative because they process information mostly through hearing and speaking. To make their points, visually impaired people frequently use hand gestures and very detailed language when speaking. Kinesthetic learners could find it difficult to comprehend concepts unless they are applied practically.

The Effects of Submodalities on Relationships

Putting together the ideal connection strategy might be quite helpful. For those of us in managerial positions, it can help forge closer bonds with colleagues, increase influence and trust with superiors, and improve communication and comprehension with subordinates. Knowing how to get through to someone when the stakes are high and proper knowledge transfer is very important, so the communication strategy must be adjusted accordingly.

Finding someone's favoritesubmodality can be a great way to energize romantic and non-romantic relationships. Many of us may know about The Five Love Languages, which explores this idea. In summary, presents, time spent together, affirmations, acts of devotion, and physical touch are all being given to the five languages. Observe a link? Every NLP submodality has a corresponding mapping, and our responses to love reveal a lot about the submodalities we value most.

A loving gesture is a kind of communication that aims to ensure that the message delivered and the message received are the same. If two individuals are unaware of each other's inclinations, they could find it difficult to communicate on the same wavelength even when they have distinct preferred submodalities. Individuals with kinesthetic inclinations are inherently more likely to respond to physical touch as their love language. At the same time, those with auditory tendencies are more likely to respond to words of affirmation. When these two combine, there may be a significant gap. The latter feels overwhelmed when the former gives her embraces and holds her hands, asking herself why she never responds, "I love you." The former asks why he never throws his arms around her at night when the latter expresses his appreciation for her in everyday life. Each attempts to communicate their love in their language, but they are not grasping the partner's most significant submodality.

The same principle holds for platonic relationships in addition to romantic ones. We need to recognize which friends and peers need verbal affirmations and appreciation, which need hugs and handshakes of congratulations, which need simple yet heartfelt gifts, and which need visual cues like posters. Lastly, having a good understanding of your preferences facilitates better need fulfillment by enabling you to express your requirements to others. Submodalities are a strong and adaptable idea, as we can see.

Prioritizing The Most Important Matters

NLP , or neuro-linguistic programming, sounds like a difficult concept for anyone to understand. Since its introduction by Richard Brandler and John Grinder in the 1970s, this idea has gained enormous popularity among modern psychologists; nonetheless, there isn't much literature available to help people who most need it. Yes, those like you should be able to access it.

NLP : What is it?

So, just what is this psychological word all about? Simply put, NLP is a technique designed to give you a sense of mental control. It was also designed to help you understand that many things could happen to you and that these occurrences could significantly impact how you view the world. Things that you might normally connect with happiness, fear, or pain have different meanings for other people. When you give it some thought, your approach to life can greatly impact how you interpret these experiences.

By giving you the chance to once again define what your surroundings mean to you, NLP aims to assist you in addressing how you process your life and surroundings. It also awakens you to the fact that you have actual power over certain bodily functions and vice versa. It tells you that your emotions and, eventually, your decisions can be influenced by how your body acts.

Being a social being, you impact those around you by behaving in the space you occupy. The same holds for the individual who chooses to communicate with you. You can easily affect others around you with your actions when you attempt to view things from a wider viewpoint. You must first understand yourself and control yourself to utilize that innate talent.

Why Become an NLP Master?

You may think this is a brilliant idea: you can completely control your life if you can masterfully control your thoughts. As they say, perspective affects most things in life. You may take control of your actions and affect the people you interact with by making a big change in how you see yourself interacting with the world.

NLP is included in business and leadership courses for this reason. It is also included in all human resource programs and seminars on salesmanship. More individuals are looking for the simplest methods to understand each NLP strategy. But there are also several in this book that you would find highly relevant to day-to-day living. Thus, think of this as one of the most crucial shortcuts to comprehending and applying the study of contemporary psychology to your own life. This was also written to make it much simpler to research and observe your interactions and behavior. More significantly, this is meant to let you know that you can broaden your perspectives, enabling you to create your roadmap for better life choices.

In the end, remember that you are learning NLP to become a better person and to discover abilities that have been latent within you for years. You may have been walking the same road for as long as you can remember, but if you pay close attention, you will see that many of the shops and residences on your street have been there for a long time. This was something Brandler mentioned in one of his lectures. You will learn the truth about your life by looking more closely at what is happening around and within you. This is the day you begin your journey of self-improvement and self-discovery through probing.

How To Acquire NLP Knowledge

First and foremost, you must remember that your actions may differ greatly from your thoughts, words, or beliefs. For this reason, practicing NLP is the greatest approach to acquiring it. For this reason, this book will require you to do several tasks to acquire new abilities or fully arm yourself with the necessary mental weapons.

First, NLP considers that individuals are not the same as they were when they were born. You are aware that your anxieties were unfounded until experience taught you to feel the way you do. However, your notions of insecurity and negative behavior are not products of the day you were born. They are all involved in the process of transformation. Remember that these unconscious lessons you have acquired might be reprogrammed to serve different purposes.

From now on, consider your map blank, with additional highways and landmarks appearing as you continue to look at it. But as you advance, periodically consult your map; you'll see that new roads and buildings will appear out of nowhere. Which path will you now choose to accomplish your objectives? You can draw your paths on this blank map as long as they serve your needs, so if you're trying to reconstruct your thoughts, actions, or even emotions, take note.

Mind Control Techniques

Everybody wants to be in charge of their daily circumstances. What most people want is to be able to control what happens. While perfection is unattainable, there exist methods that enable you to attain the intended outcomes more frequently. If you were unaware of this, it is possible to affect someone's behavior directly by sending signals and simple behaviors to them. The following advice can be used in meetings with your supervisor, during a job interview, or even with that romantic interest!

1. Sincere Grin

You should be aware that one of the most crucial and fundamental components of body language is a grin, but can you smile perfectly? Since some smiles are aggressive and forceful, you should try to communicate the truth. So, how can we make the most of this action? It's easy, really; just maintain your usual expression and extend a warm greeting and a genuine smile to the person in a matter of seconds. The individual with the biggest smile can exert more emotional power over the other person, making them feel more at ease in his presence.

2. Examine

Do not be afraid to approach the person you are interested in if they are in your group of friends. The glance will grab your attention instead of the conversation's topic of discussion, despite your natural desire to focus on what is being spoken. You will eventually draw the other person's attention when you gaze at them. You'll rapidly be able to attract their attention if you know how to assess your appearance. Whether you're at a job interview or conversing with your supervisor, focus on their eyes! This will make them more likely to feel sympathetic and confident toward you!

3. Exercise Insistency

Your ability to convince your pals will astound you. The adage "A lie repeated a thousand times becomes true" has previously been mentioned, right? However, even though we are not talking about falsehoods, you can still use this expression in the current method. If you want them to accept and trust what you say, insist on their viewpoint. Consider the scenario where you are trying to sell a product and need to demonstrate why it is a worthwhile investment. Repeating the same arguments to persuade your buyer will just make you seem inconvenient. Rather, aim to include more positive elements to establish your reputation; this will help you succeed.

4. Excuses

You might be surprised to hear that justifying your requests helps persuade the other person to grant you the desired favor. In an experiment, a lady visited five sites by saying, "Could you pick up the five pages of Xerox for me?" People refused to reply to her request in sixty percent of the cases. The identical test was then administered solely with the excuse, "I have so much work here that I will not be able to arrive on time," around 94% of the participants complied with the request right away! Make sure to provide a reason for your request the next time you have to make one!

5. Close Bonds

According to studies, tightening ties is one of the most effective ways to exert influence over another individual. A person can be quickly subdued by making them feel comfortable in your presence or by engaging their emotions. Researchers have shown that doing anything together ultimately leads to developing an emotional bond; although it may seem difficult initially, it's very easy. You can discover songs you both like together and share your music selections, for instance. They will feel more a part of you as a result!

6. Pay Attention More

You will likely succeed with this strategy if you are introverted and shy. However, you should not fear if you are a more talkative person. According to studies, those who pay closer attention to others during social or professional settings eventually take on a position of authority over them. When confronted with a challenging circumstance, attempt to maintain composure and pay attention to what the other person says. You should anticipate them asking for your input. It will be simpler to conduct a nice discussion at these moments since you will have the caller's full focus. Using this tactic will boost your credibility and elevate your viewpoint to the forefront of any conversation.

7. Be Honest

Little lies can potentially cause more harm than good; did you know that? Demonstrate to others around you that you have a strong enough personality to say the truth, even when it hurts, and that your existence is not built on making up stories to appease others. If you are truthful, you can handle the issue far more simply than if you lie and then stumble.

Utilize the Past to Shape Someone's Future

Do you know how much your upbringing has shaped who you are today? Have you observed that a person's present talents, as well as their concerns and limitations, are influenced by the way their parents and instructors shaped their childhood? These days, the outcome is nearly mathematical. We can even apply the formula: influence equals parents + our education.

Do you need some real-world instances to prove this? Nothing illustrates the impact of our education's positive and negative impact more clearly than the numerical challenges. The numbers in this position stand for the worries we had to confront and conquer with our parents' assistance. It stands for the attitudes and behaviors that we are most afraid to adopt and partake in. Therefore, how our parents and teachers handled these issues when we were kids may tell us whether to regard them as a source of dread or a behavioral difference in the present.

Therefore, it is worthwhile to delve into the past and comprehend the potential implications of the knowledge you obtained for your current situation.

NLP's Ethical Applications

The need to accomplish precise results and objectives drives the application of these strategies. Manipulating someone for your benefit or personal gain is unethical. Nonetheless, manipulation is legitimate and required in a business or organization to accomplish a shared objective.

The following are some morally acceptable methods of coercing someone to accomplish a shared good objective:

Through exerting influence. It is possible to persuade someone by manipulation so they do something they would not normally be willing to do. It is a popular tool leaders use to put pressure on their subordinates. Using this influencing strategy will help them get the desired outcome.

Through convincing. Conflicts between juniors and leaders are constant. Some leaders use this tactic to influence their peers or subordinates to change their perspectives. Instead of attempting to coerce or intimidate the subordinate into adopting their viewpoint, they give them a chance to present their case and give them a chance to change their mind.

Through motivating. When you inspire someone, you compel them to act or experience something, particularly something positive. You can motivate those around you using manipulative leadership when applied correctly. For example, you might be assigned a lengthy and challenging project in the upcoming months. You are meant to have a few small initiatives here and there to gain your partners' trust.

Develop Your Manipulating Skills

This entails honing your abilities and fostering them over time to make them appropriate for your goals. The most difficult aspect of manipulation is learning to become an expert and get others to feel like you do. You may take an acting class to strengthen your persuasive skills.

Comparing and contrasting is another method for improving your abilities. You can mimic or copy their body language, intonation style, and other traits via pacing. For example, you can mimic your boss's tone of voice and body language, such as how they sit, to persuade them to give you a raise. Additionally, it has been discovered that, particularly in a professional context, it is simpler to persuade people when you are composed than when you are upset.

You ought to exude charisma at all times. People with charming personalities are said to constantly manage to achieve what they want. To elicit conversation, you should always project an accessible smile and brighten the atmosphere with your body language. You need to be able to converse with people of all ages, from your eight-year-old sister to your university professor.

Develop your people reading skills. Every human is distinct and different in some way. It's important to take your time teaching someone, figuring out the best way to approach them, and determining what makes them want to comply with your demands before you make your first attempt at manipulation.

Rethink Patterns To Direct People's Thoughts In The Way You Desire

Imagine a conversation in which you discuss something, but in reality, you would prefer to discuss something else. Let's refer to the intended topic as "B" and the actual topic as "A." The following pattern may help you reframe the direction of your conversation: "The problem isn't 'A,' it's 'B,' and that means..."

One of the greatest things about this redefined pattern is that it requires no thought or preparation. It can be used to change the subject of any discussion. Combined with the method of asking questions we studied in the previous chapter, this strategy becomes even more potent. For instance: "What is it about your production equipment that is causing the problems in quality? The issue is not about the quantity you are producing, but how your company is not producing quality products."

When you pose this issue, imagine that the group's attention will change from quantity to quality. The nice part is that it will occur quite subtly.

"The fact that the equipment is old is a problem, but the bigger issue is how seriously the quality control staff is taking their jobs...and how well the managers are communicating their vision to the staff," someone else might say once the group has begun discussing quality.

You can alter the discussion's course in multiple ways using this technique.

Proof: Redefining Work Patterns

Redefining patterns is a successful NLP impact strategy, according to RintuBasu's 2009 paper.

A Brief Narrative

I was required to lead a focus group in my company to discuss management-employee communication issues. Organizing a focus group might be challenging.

It is very simple for a group of coworkers to become sidetracked and lose focus when they are acquainted with one another. Many HR hours are lost, and no useful insights are frequently obtained from the focus group.

Whenever it felt like the group was straying from the desired topic, I used the redefine pattern to get the conversation back on track. When a conversation seemed to be dragging on a certain subject, I also used the redefine pattern to move to more worthwhile subjects.

For example, at one point, the group should have discussed methods to enhance communication between management and staff. Still, instead, they spent more than ten minutes talking about a problem with management policies. "What measures can we take to improve communication? The issue is not about the problems in policies, but how we communicate the problems that we encounter to the higher management," I interrupted.

In this manner, the focus group came to insightful findings and determined the appropriate course of action.

The Reasons for Learning to Redefine Patterns

First, you should understand basic patterns to transition any conversation from one topic to another.

Second, you can utilize the redefine pattern when arguing with someone, and you want to move on from their point of contention, but they are stuck on it.

Thirdly, you can utilize it in sales to counter customer arguments and instead discuss the product's advantages.

Finally, you should understand how to reframe patterns to get someone to date you. You want them to think about how amazing it would be, not how much of a scandal it would make.

What You Should Understand Initially About Redefine Patterns

You may use redefined patterns to nudge any conversation in your desired direction. Before you begin redefining patterns, you should understand a few things.

Though you are free to alter the topic and take the discussion in whatever direction, it is best to do so gradually. Making a bold move could turn off your viewers.

It is best to employ redefine patterns when you are in a position of authority.

Redefining patterns can be effectively conducted in group talks.

Chapter 2: Master Your Language Ability

Understanding the power of words is the first and most important step toward becoming a master of persuasion. Many of us are ignorant of the power of words over other people or the signals we send to them.

You must first recognize and comprehend the incredible power concealed in your words to develop into a persuasive person who can use words to manipulate everyone around you. You may simply influence somebody in whatever way you choose by doing something as basic as using the appropriate words and speaking tone.

There are countless incredible things that language can enable you to accomplish.

The Diary of a Young Girl by Anne Frank

I think this wonderful book by Anne Frank is the most important and well-read Holocaust literature. Anne Frank kept a private journal throughout this time. She was not too old at that point.

At the age of 15, she passed away in a concentration camp. Her father obtained her diaries after her passing and had them published. The book/diary recounts Anne's Holocaust experience and her efforts to maintain normalcy despite the seeming total darkness surrounding her.

Readers of all ages can readily read and understand the novel because of its charming, youthful perspective. This little book made a big difference in subsequent generations' comprehension of the Holocaust, the thoughts of a young girl experiencing it, and the thoughts of other young children like Anne.

An Account of Frederick Douglass's Life

Another illustration of how language and literature have a powerful influence on how people think is seen in the work of Frederick Douglass. Among the most well-liked abolitionists of all time is Frederick Douglass.

This remarkable man, formerly a slave, educated himself to become free and even discussed the subject with Abraham Lincoln. He became well-known very quickly for his persuasive oratory abilities. But he chose to write a book when some people questioned whether he had been a slave, in part due to his gifted writing.

His work became one of the most-read first-hand stories of slavery of that era and became one of the most well-known and best-selling narratives written by a slave. Many people were able to release themselves from slavery because of the book.

You know the power of words if you have read these books or heard someone discuss them. Because these novels skillfully employed persuasive techniques to appeal to people's emotions, they altered people's perceptions and the course of history.

These books, along with many more like them, use hypnotic language designed to hypnotize readers through the power of words. You, too, may learn this talent if you have this guide. But first, what is hypnotic language?

Hypnotic language is a form of NLP (Neuro-linguistic programming) approach. NLP is a language, programming, and psychotherapy method established by John Grinder and Richard Bandler.

Now that you realize how beneficial persuasive talents are, your first step to becoming a master of persuasion is to imagine yourself as a powerful orator who effortlessly convinces and effectively achieves intentions and goals. Think of this scenario for a while until it becomes strong. Write down details of your vision and any reflections or emotions that come up while you practice this exercise. This will help to solidify your intention. Don't skip this step! This simple action step will help place the suggestions in your subconscious mind that you will become a great persuader.

What Does The Dark Triad Aspect Look Like In People?

According to evidence from several academic research studies, people with dark-triad personalities appear marginally better than average at first appearance. This is because although those with dark triad characteristics put more care into how they look, the difference in beauty vanishes when they "dress up" for the house and forgo makeup. Most people agree that narcissistic actors are the most attractive.

A Psycholog's Suggestion: A Dark Triad of Characteristics

We would like to remind you that none of our publications on psychology, including those with the headline "psychologist's consultation," are intended to be used as a substitute for in-person counseling or as a psychology textbook. Our publications aim to increase awareness of psychology and improve interpersonal understanding among readers, including prospective clients and working psychologists. It is more beneficial to speak with a reputable psychologist if you want to receive professional psychological assistance.

Counsel from a psychologist. We were consulted by a couple that came in. Allow me to present an imagined yet realistic conversation. "Over the years of living with my wife, I realized she was a boundless woman and a narcissistic schemer," he declared. Moreover, he is a narcissist! The psychologist: "Let's calm down and talk about such a phenomenon as the dark triad of personality."

A brief history of the concept of the "dark triad of personality" 's introduction into psychology

It was not until lately that the dark triad of personality was discussed in psychology. However, this unofficial, non-academic idea quickly gained traction among psychologists who worked as consultants and psychotherapists. A dark triad—an intriguing name—had a significant role. It seems to be!

In 2002, DelroyPaulhus and Kevin Williams, two Canadian psychologists at the University of British Columbia, proposed that combining the three psychological traits of narcissism, psychopathy, and Machiavellianism in one individual results in a completely new psychological attribute. Put differently; it exceeds 3. A new phenomenon known as the "dark triad of personality" arises when narcissism, psychopathy, and Machiavellianism combine and interact in an individual's psyche. The simple mathematical sum of its component parts cannot explain this phenomenon.

What was the origin of the name? The reason it's called the triad is that it has three parts. Dark because the negative aspects of human nature are brought to light and intensified in this phenomenon.

Without a doubt, the adjective "dark" is an evaluation. It has a low rating. What, then, did Kevin Williams and DelroyPaulhus mean? They believe that a person with a dark triangle personality is characterized by a tendency to lie, manipulate, and take advantage of others, as well as a sense of superiority, a contempt for socially accepted norms of behavior, social dominance, egocentrism, selfishness, insensitivity to the problems of others, ill will, lack of empathy, and emotional coldness.

The University of British Columbia provided these psychologists' ideas to other psychologists as well as psychologists-practitioners. Why? One explanation for this is that, by 2002, many people felt that the typological approach to personality that was then used in psychology was too restrictive.

The typological method describes a person's personality using a very small set of fundamental psychological characteristics. Various accounts vary on how many there are—between one and two dozen. Just! Decisive tests with established validity, reliability, and consistency are used to diagnose these fundamental psychological traits. Some conditional scores are used to express test results. Every psychological attribute is assigned a numerical value.

Next, various personality types were gathered from a dozen or more fundamental psychological attributes represented in digital indications, such as the cubes of the building. That summarizes the typological approach to personality in psychology in its most basic form.

Consultant psychologists and psychologist-psychotherapists have observed, meanwhile, that the academic typological method does not accurately capture an individual's true personality. Academic personality types are insufficient since personality types are significantly more diverse in real life. Therefore, many psychologists welcomed the discovery of a novel type that wasn't boiled down to a straightforward arithmetic sum of previously understood psychological features. Ultimately, a practical psychologist's job most often involves accurately assessing the client's personality. This personality type chooses psychological training, psychotherapy, or counseling appropriately. Many psychologists who aspire to be effective work in this manner; they want to genuinely assist the client and then take accountability for their work. The dark trio of personality was a novel idea that helped the psychologist solve the psychological issues it raised by describing certain individuals very realistically.

However, as experience proved, the dark triad of personality frequently results in greater issues for both the psychologist and the person with these traits nearby. Even the same person with a dark triad personality type does not always feel particularly uncomfortable psychologically.

The dark triangle of an individual's psyche presents a gambler's dilemma for a psychologist and a difficulty for the person's loved ones. Many psychologists believe that an individual with a dark triad has an underlying psychological issue that causes internal discord and interpersonal difficulties. Even though, in our experience, psychological issues are more common in the close relationships of such individuals—they are concerned, searching for explanations, offended, and furious, as well as seeking novel approaches to the individual and innovative forms of psychological support. The very bearer of psychological traits, referred to as the "dark triad of personality," generally leads a fairly psychologically tolerable and occasionally even comfortable life; nothing in his life is unchangeable, and he in particular, but he also plays a major role in inducing negative emotions in those close to him. He continues, asking, "What did I do? It was they that had such an odd reaction."

In our hypothetical but realistic conversation about a psychologist's session. Typically, a dark triad only affects one partner or one member of a large family. After all, the most prevalent psychological diagnosis is not the dark triad of personality. It is highly unlikely that he will be with two family members simultaneously.

Now, let's take a closer look at the dark triad of personality, including what it is, how it shows up in behavior, what psychological symptoms it carries, the effects it has on the individual and his surroundings, and how a psychologist can help.

Learn more about the signs of the dark triad of personality in psychology.

The dark triad of personality refers to at least three psychological traits (hence the name—triad) in the human psyche that interact to create a particular personality type exhibited in behavior. These qualities include psychopathy, Machiavellianism, and narcissism. To diagnose an individual with a dark triad personality disorder, three requirements must be met:

This person possesses the psychological traits of psychopathy, Machiavellianism, and narcissism all at the same time. They must be found and validated by stringent psychodiagnostic techniques, such as a series of conclusive personality tests.

The expression of these three psychological traits in the human psyche is not so strong as to already correlate with the symptoms of a clinical mental illness. The dark triad of personality, a corresponding psychiatric diagnostic, is more frequent than a psychological (lighter) diagnosis. The person's dark triangle deviates from the mental standard. Keep this in mind as we discuss the typical behavior of the dark triad carrier.

The high degree of accentuation or personality disorder already corresponds to the expression of all three of these psychological qualities in the human mind. A person is mentally normal even though his psychological responses and behavior do not match the conventional ideas of sufficiency.

Chapter 2: Operation

You may start to comprehend how NLP functions now that you have a basic understanding of its history and definition. The three primary tenets of NLP are learning subjectivity and consciousness. These ideas, then, fall under the general heading of mental communication retraining and involve that process.

Subjectivity

Every encounter we have is unique. This implies that no two people have precisely the same experiences. Since every individual's experience is unique and based on their own particular beliefs, feelings, thoughts, and so on, no two experiences are alike. Depending on a person's background, gender, traumas, personal history, and other experiences that shape their conscious reality, two people may perceive the same piece of art quite differently.

Our minds search internally for past experiences to draw comparisons between the current experience and previous experiences we have experienced before when we gaze outward. We draw many connections and associations from our memories that guide our cognitive processes and worldviews to the present.

Our five senses and the words we use to think about and explain our experiences form a big part of our experiences. When two individuals look at the same painting, for instance, their experiences will differ because one of them notices something in the lower left corner that makes them think of their first house's smell, as well as the appearance and feel of that space. This allows them to associate the painting with a sensory memory. Our senses shape our experiences, and while our mechanical abilities may permit us to function identically, our conscious identities prevent us from knowing the same thing in the same way twice.

Being Aware

This is your level of experience-awareness. You are aware of your experiences, ego, thoughts, and feelings. It is awareness of your interior self and the people, things, and surroundings around you.

When looking at a painting there, you can tell you are in an art museum because you decided to visit that particular day. You know that you and other viewers are gazing upon a work of art. You are happy that you brought your jumper because you are aware of the little drop in temperature. You know that the painting you are looking at has a specific style and background and a specific size, shape, color, and texture. In addition, you start to become conscious of how this specific picture makes you feel, what it makes you think of, how long it has been since you have enjoyed viewing excellent art in a museum, and how much you have missed the opportunity to do so.

Your consciousness always shapes your experiences. It is a jumble of perceptions, emotions, ideas, and personal interpretations of the current instant you find yourself. Our unconscious thinking and conscious behavior are closely related. As you may remember from earlier in the text, many of our thoughts and emotions that we are unaware of are stored in the unconscious. This is the domain of our anxieties, fears, doubts, mental processes, and early training. Unknowingly, these unconscious patterns influence our conscious existence.

Therefore, even though you are enjoying that painting at the moment, conscious of all its qualities, and aware of your subjective reaction to it, you might not know how your feelings about the experience are connected to deeper meanings and behaviors. For example, you might not have realized that you have avoided art museums for so long. Despite your deep desire to become a professional painter, you dropped out of art school because your family convinced you it was impossible to succeed as an artist.

There are countless instances of how our conscious and unconscious minds interact to shape our subjective perceptions; this is just one example.

Acquiring knowledge

Learning is acquired by imitating what others have already accomplished, demonstrated, investigated, experienced, developed, and so on. The science of radioactivity was discovered and pioneered by Marie Curie. She attended a university to study science and absorbed the discoveries made by others before her, which were incorporated into our shared understanding of science. She then used what she had discovered to further her research and deepen her science comprehension. She had to go through the procedures more than once to achieve the accuracy she needed when trying to extract the substance of her research and as a result.

The key idea here is that learning occurs when one imitates actions that produce a desired outcome. It's referred to as "modeling" in NLP . When you emulate someone else's actions, you pick up their behavior to accomplish a favorable outcome. If someone is knowledgeable about the science of radioactivity, you can use their techniques to implement them to get the intended outcomes. Even though none of us are pioneers, we may benefit from their experiences.

Breaking the patterns and loops we have been conditioned to run continuously involves breaking through with NLP by learning to model behaviors that reframe our thinking to become more positive and engineer a new approach to our lives.

Step 2: Make Inquiries

"How many individuals converse in the same language even when they do not speak it?"

Russell Hoban

By posing questions, you can obtain very crucial information. Get your prospect to start a conversation once you have built rapport. Here, you want to learn as much as you can about your potential customers.

Usually, I like to begin an interview with questions that are specifically about the interviewee's business. Said another way, I'm interested in learning more about them and their work. I'm trying to gauge whether they might be in need of my goods or services. I'll usually ask, "What do you do?" or "What are you interested in?" I do have an interest in them at this point. Once we've built a connection, it makes sense for me to want to learn more about the needs of my prospect.

I can then offer them the greatest suggestions for resolving their issue because I care about their circumstances.

I usually ask the opposite questions of them. I'll ask: "Why do you want my product/services?" In these circumstances, the prospect will frequently start to defend you. They'll say things such as, "Well, I was thinking of attending your seminar because I need to sell more, or I'm going to get fired."

Let's say a potential client phones to inquire about my seminars or coaching, and I launch into a sales pitch about the advantages I believe he should know about. I feel as though I'm playing crap. Perhaps I'll be fortunate. Perhaps I won't. So why should I place a wager? Not when it comes to closing a deal, anyway. I'm interested in the inside scoop. Simply inquire. People are happy to tell you. Their goal is to resolve their issues. I swear.

You can uncover the prospect's internal success narrative by probing them with questions. I am aware that sounds a little difficult. However, figuring out your client's internal definition of success is just asking your prospect what he imagines his life will be like if your product or service doesn't fix the issue. As you try to convince a potential customer to buy an automobile, you might think he wants to impress the girls. After going through your entire sales pitch, you try to close the deal by saying something like, "Just picture what the ladies will think of you when you're driving this car."

What would happen if your prospect's wife was extremely envious and would lose her mind if she caught sight of her husband? It appears that your potential customer was searching for a vehicle with a strong safety record the entire time. You've just dissuaded him from buying from you. Not very intelligent. Your prospect's internal success representation is something you can never know. We can't open his mind, peer inside, and say, "Oh, this is what he's thinking," so it's difficult to know. You must inquire.

Compare that circumstance to this one. You will quickly learn that your potential customer is searching for a vehicle with an excellent safety record. This makes it simple to give him what he wants to see, give him that sense of security, and end the conversation with what he wants to hear. Asking, "What is important to you in an XYZ?" is the simplest method to learn what a prospect is searching for. "How would you know when that problem is solved?" is another pertinent query.

As previously stated, when you ask questions of your prospect, you are attempting to ascertain which principal representation system they use. This is connected to the predicates discussed in Step 1's writing. Find out what kinds of terms your prospect uses when you speak with them. Do they have a strong visual component, like sight, look, or visualize? Or do they primarily employ tactile terms like grab, feel, and concrete? An uncommon type is auditory, in which a potential client might say things like "sounds," "rings a bell," or "resonates." Or is the potential customer utilizing a collection of systems, including auditory digital terms like perceive, recognize, or comprehend? A whole new universe of possibilities becomes available when you customize your representation to your prospects.

People see the world differently, which is why this has a significant impact. I know it's incredible, but if you are trying to sell a car to a prospect who is very visual. You start talking about how the leather is soft, the engine purrs, and the acceleration feels great; chances are he won't be interested. You will speak to him in his language as you explain the features, colors, and pictures he will see as he speeds down the street. It's not as though your visual prospect is blind to those other details. He merely values the visual cues more than they do.

Never undervalue this. It has a profound impact. You will quickly close a deal if you begin explaining your good or service like your potential customer sees the world. Feel free to give it a try on yourself. Play back the audio and video of you discussing your product in a primarily visual, aural, kinesthetic, and auditory format. It's going to sound better on one of the four. The same thing is going to happen to your prospect. It's best when there's no guesswork involved. You only need to consider what he says to determine which predicates to employ. Make sure the questions you pose are framed in the dominant digital representation system—visual, auditory, kinesthetic, or auditory—for your prospect.

Here are a few instances:

"What does a good training seminar look like to you?"

"How could one tell when a training session felt perfect?" or "What is it that just feels right about a good training?"

"What did you really resonate with at the last training you attended?"

"What particular aspect of the training gives you that common sense? "What profound insight are you hoping to gain from this training?"

It is simpler for people to respond "Yes" when you ask them questions in their native tongue. Even though your prospects speak English, when you don't use the same phrases they do, you're forcing them to translate into a new way of seeing the world.

You can even discover your prospect's purchasing plan if you have the time. Find out how your prospect purchased a product or service comparable to yours the last time. You might also inquire about their method of purchasing a piece of apparel. Since they most likely go through the same procedures every time they make a purchase, you're curious about the actions they used to obtain that good or service. Therefore, if you can guide them through the same process again, they will inevitably purchase your good or service since it seems, feels, or sounds right.

I use the following queries to put this method into practice: "So Mr. Prospect, the last time you bought a car, did you just go to the dealer, see something you like, and buy it, or did you do your research first and then go looking?" Individuals are nearly always fairly transparent about their particular purchasing process. They frequently take great pride in their purchasing approach. Asking them about the most recent good or service they used is another tactic I like to use. I'll also inquire about something they received a fantastic bargain on.

Pay attention to what they have to say. Do they act on impulse, do some research, determine whether they need it, and then buy it, or are they the kind that simply sees something, wants it, and buys it? They will tell you if you listen carefully.

Lastly, you want to learn about the prospect's approach to reassurance. How does your potential customer know he made a wise purchase? Does his friends and family tell him, or does he intuitively know he has a positive feeling or image in his head? Try inquiring, "How can you tell when a purchase is good?" or "Tell me about a service or product you purchased that satisfied you." As an illustration, "I know you truly appreciated that car you own. How could you be sure you had made the appropriate purchase?" Additionally, note whether the prospect informs you that they purchased the incorrect one, and make sure your offering is unrelated to this notion.

After the deal is concluded, you should follow up with the prospect to ensure they are still happy with the purchase by using this reassuring technique. Thus, if the potential customer responds, "Everyone I know says I got a great deal," Remember this. Tell the prospect that his friends will all agree that he received a wonderful deal once he accepts your offer. A potential customer indicates that he values his friends' opinions when he tells you that they reassured him. Saying anything insignificant to him, like "You can see you got a great deal, can't you?" is not a good idea. He requires confirmation from an outside source that he can rely on. It won't work to ask this prospect if he feels he got a decent deal. Had the potential customer said, "It just seemed right to me, so I know I got a good deal,"

Then you can be sure he's conjuring up a vivid image in his head. There is no requirement for outside validation for this prospect. For this prospect, a straightforward "You can see you got a great deal, can't you?" will suffice.

Recall that you have a rapport with your prospect and that it is normal to ask inquiries. This is a convo that flows naturally. Return to step one if you don't feel like you are on the same page. Step two will become a lot simpler and more organic as a result.

You can finish step two in a minute or two or take as much time as necessary. The duration is contingent upon the potential customer and the product being offered. Be thorough, take notes, and refer to them anytime you interact with your client to build a long-term relationship with someone who will buy from you repeatedly. You'll know immediately what to say to make their purchases from you as simple as feasible. By making it simple for your prospect to buy from you, you're doing them a huge favor. Many consumers are afraid they will experience buyer's regret. Your prospect's concern will be lessened after you ascertain their particular reassurance approach and can offer it to them. Well done! Never forget that you are helping your prospect. If they don't require your goods or service, we'll quickly find out, and we can break up amicably. If circumstances change, this may lead to a referral or two and establish the foundation for a future partnership.

Techniques for Neurological Programming

Before delving into NLP techniques, it is important to comprehend the contexts in which they are applied. Most of these circumstances have psychological underpinnings. This indicates that rather than affecting a person's physical or mental aspects, the events handled by NLP mostly affect their psychological component. These circumstances include extreme melancholy, which is commonly referred to as depression, and difficulty making decisions, which is commonly referred to as someone who is highly indecisive about issues. This occurs when someone is reluctant to move forward when it is necessary for their well-being or the well-being of others. A second scenario is when someone experiences extreme mood fluctuations. While mood swings are rather common, they can become harmful when they occur more frequently and in greater quantities. This means that to overcome them, one needs psychological assistance. Thus, the psychological and exhaustion of the victim's mind are the conditions appropriate for NLP.

NLP strategies are sensible to use and are exact and comprehensive. The following are a few of the tactics explained in great depth so that you, the reader, may grasp them.

First, NLP is used for individuals whose issues are immediate. The issue must be present for someone to read their brain waves or for a psychiatrist to read them. The issue must appear or be able to materialize. The professional should be able to successfully address the issue with the aid of the brain waves as well as the indicators and symptoms. The presence of the problem is crucial in unraveling the enigma and its related problems. If brain waves are present, they aid in keeping everything under control and manageable. This further contributes to the brain wave read's simplicity and clarity.

Being conscious of one's surroundings is another tactic that may help one understand oneself and, more importantly, be frank and unbiased while discussing concerns. Brain waves indicate what is being read when a person is mentally clear. In contrast to when their thoughts are clear and tranquil, people with messy minds do not see things well. For this method to be effective, individuals must also be free of negative thoughts and physical ailments. This is an extremely practical and life-applicable method.

For NLP to be effective, the patient and psychiatrist's speaking and listening abilities must be flawless. A patient and physician or expert should have a positive and understanding relationship. The specialist needs to imagine themselves in other people's or the patient's shoes. This aims to facilitate confidence between the patient and the experts. This facilitates the patient's opening up and allows the professionals to treat them. This could become an issue if the patient is closed off, making it difficult for the specialist to diagnose and treat the issue at hand. Thus, a relationship between the patient and the professional must exist to maintain order.

For NLP to solve a problem, the expert must identify the issue. How is it possible? This might happen when a professional observes and interprets the symptoms and strange behavior that the patients present. The specialists will be able to address the issue once they have gained clarity on identifying the symptoms. Things get simpler and easier as a result. Finding the problem promptly and building more confidence between the victim and the expert depends on detection.

After detection, applying what is known comes next. Using the knowledge one has acquired from their patient to assist them with their concerns and problems. To help their patient overcome obstacles and challenges, specialists must make the most of the knowledge they have about their patients. This is a fantastic method for handling people's psychological issues. Not only do psychiatrists utilize this technique, but educators and other professionals do as well. This is an excellent approach that should always be used when the problem has been identified.

Ultimately, psychological issues are manageable. The patient's issues might be resolved quickly if they are open to accepting change in their lives. Every issue has a simple fix. It takes gratitude and willingness for someone to accept change in their lives. There is no other way to make things straightforward. Also, life needs to be straightforward. It must be trouble-free to be beneficial and healthy. This is the ideal approach for everyone to live and experience complete happiness.

The techniques assist one or more people in solving all of their issues. All of the techniques accomplished make it easier and faster for the experts to finish their work. To maintain order and safety, strategies are established for protocols and guidelines. There are solutions for every psychological issue. To provide a clear understanding of what NLP is and how it operates, I have just highlighted a handful of the many tactics that are used in NLP . It functions simply and effectively. Does NLP offer any benefits or drawbacks, then? The benefits and drawbacks are distinct and easy to understand.

Enhancing Academic Performance

In the previous exercise, you performed a process called "mapping across" images, utilizing the many characteristics of the images (known as submodalities, such as picture size) to transform perplexity into comprehension, beliefs into doubts, and similar changes.

Assuming you possess proficiency in geography but lack proficiency in French. If you have acquired knowledge in French and possess adequate data, aligning your mental representation of French with your mental representation of geography accurately (thus ensuring they share the same programming codes or submodalities) will significantly enhance your proficiency in French. Coding all subjects with the same level of proficiency and enthusiasm as your greatest or favorite subject fosters a sense of competence and enjoyment across all courses.

Suppose you derive pleasure from disseminating information or knowledge you acquired with acquaintances. In that case, you can encode the examination or test in the same way you encode sharing with friends. In this manner, exam stress or anxiety is reduced or eradicated.

3Ensure that the internal debate is identified in every instance. Ensure that the internal conversation related to French aligns with geography in terms of location and tone while expressing sentiments comparable to your remarks on geography. It is essential to address the internal dialogue throughout the exam to align it with the dialogue shared with friends.

To significantly improve your success rate, paying attention to both visual representations and interior thoughts and conversations is crucial.

As an illustration.

A 12-year-old girl takes pleasure in studying Latin but has a strong aversion towards geography. She excels in both subjects. The geography teacher frequently raises their voice. Initially, I prompted her to imagine the teacher adorned with a clown's red nose and a duck behind. This elicited her laughter and facilitated the coding process of geography, like how she codes Latin. The teacher's coding style became a meme, and it was comparatively simpler to reduce the teacher's intimidation factor than to win the girl's favor. Her performance in geography shows noticeable improvement, leading to an increased enjoyment of the studies.

Here is another instance.

A highly intelligent young man arrived to meet me before his simulated GCSE exams. I assisted him in programming all subjects by his strongest subject. The examinations were designed to mimic informal written communication with a buddy.

He achieved a perfect score of 10 As, with eight of them being awarded stars, and he replicated this outstanding result in the final exams. He exerted significant effort and likely would have achieved success independently. However, he and his parents felt the re-coding helped to attain good results.

Using Your Wants Against You

The last item that we will look at is the idea that manipulators and NLP professionals will learn how to use your wants, or the desires of their selected victim, against them. Those who are adept in applying NLP are quickly able to tell and know what they desire. This is because they have wants that are important as well. While everyone has their individual and unique experiences, ones that can keep them away from others, it isn't uncommon for many of us to share goals. Achieving fame or money or attaining true bliss might be significant ones.

You will find that manipulators adept at using NLP are practiced at knowing what people want. They can then use these urges against the victim to acquire what they seek. Remember that the manipulator can feed off their victim's emotions, and the manipulator isn't going to care how your feelings affect you, but how they can use these emotions against you. For example, they may be skilled at locating those who want more attention or seek the favor of others and then prey on them to achieve what they, the manipulator, want.

Those who can use the strategies of NLP will be more dangerous than the manipulators we discussed earlier. These individuals may take things a bit further, and they can take the time to learn how the brain works and then can use this to their benefit. If you believe that someone is utilizing these tactics of NLP against you, then you may discover that it is harder to deal with and avoid compared to conventional manipulation. Often, it is harder even to notice. But the good news is that you can continue to use the techniques we discussed earlier in this guidebook to deal with these manipulators as well.

NLP is a decorative technique that individuals can use on themselves if they are interested in learning more about themselves and changing how they think and view the world. But if these techniques are used in the hands of the manipulator, it can be a dangerous tool that is hard for the victim even to recognize, much less fight against.

How and Why Does Manipulation Work?

Despite what it may seem, manipulation is going to work efficiently. For the most part, people will be automatically wired to say no to something the first time they hear about it. This happens if whoever is asking the question is someone the victim doesn't know or trust already. When it is someone that the victim trusts, they are more likely to think about the subject, and there is a higher likelihood of them saying yes.

He achieved a perfect score of ten As in a row, with eight of them being awarded with stars. He then replicated this outstanding result in the final exams. He exerted diligent effort and likely would have achieved success independently. Nevertheless, he and his parents believed that the re-coding process significantly contributed to achieving outstanding outcomes.

Manipulating Your Desires to Control You

We will now examine the concept that manipulators and professionals in neuro-linguistic programming (NLP) acquire the ability to exploit individuals' interests or preferences to their disadvantage. Proficient practitioners of NLP can discern and ascertain their desires with ease. This is because they have significant desires. Although individuals may have distinct personal experiences that differentiate them from others, it is not unusual for many of us to have common aims. Attaining fame, money, or genuine happiness can be a significant aspiration.

Proficient manipulators skilled in the use of Neuro-Linguistic Programming possess the ability to discern individuals' desires with precision. Subsequently, they can exploit these urges to manipulate the victim into fulfilling their objectives. It is important to note that the manipulator is capable of exploiting the emotions of their target, and they are indifferent to the impact of these emotions on the target's well-being. Instead, the manipulator focuses on how they might leverage these emotions to their advantage. For instance, they may possess a skill for identifying individuals who crave further attention or seek validation from others and subsequently exploit them to obtain their desired outcomes.

Individuals proficient in Neuro-Linguistic Programming (NLP) strategies will possess a greater threat level than the previously discussed manipulators. These individuals can delve deeper into the subject matter and dedicate time to comprehensively understand the brain's functioning. Subsequently, they can effectively utilize this knowledge to benefit themselves. Suppose you perceive someone using these techniques of Neuro-Linguistic Programming (NLP) to manipulate you. In that case, you may discover that it is more challenging to confront and evade than conventional manipulation, and it is often even more difficult to identify. However, the positive aspect is that you can persist in employing the identical strategies previously discussed in this guidebook to effectively handle those who engage in such manipulative behavior.

NLP, or Neuro-Linguistic Programming, is a self-applied technique that allows individuals to get deeper insights into their thoughts and perspectives, enabling them to change their cognitive processes and worldview. However, when employed by a manipulator, these skills can become a difficult instrument, posing a formidable challenge for the victim to identify, let alone combat.

What are the mechanisms and reasons behind the effectiveness of manipulation?

Contrary to appearances, manipulation will be quite effective. Generally, individuals are instinctively inclined to reject something upon initial exposure. If the person asking the question is unfamiliar or untrusted by the victim, the likelihood of the victim considering the subject and agreeing is lower. However, if the person asking is someone the victim trusts, there is a greater chance of them pondering the matter and responding affirmatively.

Suppose you are not acquainted with the other individual and have not established their trust before attempting to manipulate them. Consequently, whenever you request the other individual, they will just respond with a negative answer. The concept associated with this topic is quite straightforward. We are generally reluctant to accept items from someone we lack trust. It resembles accepting a favor from an unfamiliar person, which may render you susceptible and exposed to potential danger. These are actions that we would refrain from undertaking. When an unfamiliar or untrusted individual requests something from us, it is natural to feel inclined to refuse. This is due to our lack of confidence and familiarity with the person, which prevents us from predicting whether the outcome will be detrimental to us somehow.

This principle applies to others as well while attempting to manipulate them. Soliciting a favor from someone carries a significant likelihood of receiving a negative response unless a preexisting relationship and a foundation of trust have been established. Naturally, there are measures that you may take to expedite the development of those emotions, accelerating the attainment of a positive response. By acquiring further knowledge and honing your skills via practice, you will swiftly gain the ability to control people and elicit their agreement.

Ineffective Manipulation

A wide range of manipulation techniques are available worldwide, and we often choose to focus on the incorrect form of manipulation. This is due to the widespread exposure to manipulation through many mediums, such as literature, films, and news outlets. These sites will primarily focus on discussing manipulation and its negative consequences. How frequently have you encountered instances when a group or cult exploited individuals, or even a smaller number, and successfully induced significant alterations in their personalities and beyond, as exemplified by instances often reported on television? You may be familiar with instances where individuals exhibit a willingness to commit acts of murder, assault, or other forms of aggression after previously demonstrating exceptional composure and self-restraint.

Although it may seem excessive, there are numerous instances where manipulation is perceived as a detrimental phenomenon. Typically, this occurs when the manipulator seeks to achieve their desires or obtain personal benefits, disregarding the consequences for the other individual involved. They may also desire for the target to develop a reliance on them, ensuring the ability to repeatedly utilize that individual as desired.

The individual who is adversely affected or injured is typically the target in this scenario. Whether experiencing physical pain or being convinced of their worthlessness, individuals will discover that being targeted can have detrimental effects. The manipulator is the sole one who will derive advantages from this form of manipulation.

NLP Techniques And Strategies For Everyday Life

Utilizing Natural Language Processing (NLP) Patterns to Enhance and Intensify Emotional Responses

Consider a scenario in which you have a preferred route that you consistently take when commuting from your residence to your workplace daily. This driving routine becomes monotonous, and at times, it requires minimal exertion and focus since you are already familiar with the procedure.

It functions similarly to an autopilot system, allowing you to allocate this time to contemplate the activities you must accomplish at home, reflect on your day, and attend to other matters. At the same time, your subconscious mind handles all other responsibilities.

Instantaneously, a loud noise resonates and abruptly impacts. There is currently an obstruction in your way due to the recent falling of a sizable tree. You abruptly apply the brakes, causing the car to come to an abrupt stop with a loud screeching noise. Within the immediate moments following, you find yourself seated in your vehicle, contemplating the recent events.

Your subconscious mind is unfamiliar with this circumstance; hence, it lacks the knowledge to react appropriately. At this juncture, you must intervene; your cognitive mind must assume command and provide explicit directives on managing the situation. The subconscious mind efficiently executes automatic patterns, allowing the conscious mind to focus on things requiring conscious attention.

When attempting to modify certain patterns, automatic habits, thoughts, emotions, and actions can occasionally pose a challenge. Although you may be willing to change, your subconscious mind consistently hinders your progress, resulting in repetitive behavior.

Recognizing that the subconscious mind is highly inept at making decisions is important. Only the cognitive mind possesses the capacity to create determinations. Pattern interruption, employed as an NLP tool, compels the subconscious mind to enter a state of anticipation for input from the conscious mind.

It facilitates the process of overcoming habits and adopting new techniques and modifications. It facilitates reprogramming the subconscious mind, enabling it to act as a conduit for instructions from the conscious mind.

Patterns commonly denote the clandestine NLP tactics employed for seduction. A set of patterns achieved infamy within the seduction community and began to be recognized as the prohibited patterns. They acquired this designation because they were considered excessively gloomy and without moral principles for the community to embrace. Given their infamy, the community frequently seeks them, yet they prove elusive. The items are displayed in their entirety.

An example of such a pattern is 'the shadow and the rising sun.' It is extensively prohibited in the seduction world because it utilizes concepts from Jungian psychology to access a woman's concealed shadow, which represents her hidden and darker aspects of personality.

The seducer initiates a conversation regarding the concept of opposites. He emphasized discussing opposing imagery that can inspire the concept of gloom, such as the interplay between light and dark, day and night, and yin and yang. The individual discusses the significance of embracing the existence of a shadowy aspect, asserting its indispensability in giving purpose to life. Subsequently, he proceeds to discuss a shadowy aspect within every individual. This concept revolves around the emergence of a sun on the horizon, creating shadows and a transformative effect on one's perception of everything. The seducer, after that, entices the individual to embrace her concealed nature and perceive the world from its perspective. This renders the target vulnerable, causing them to exhibit behavior they would not normally display.

An additional strategy frequently employed in combination with the technique above is referred to as the hospital pattern. This pattern involves the seducer deliberately oscillating the emotional state of their target between intense sensations of gratification and intense sensations of distress. The fast oscillation of emotional states, occurring repeatedly, is designed to induce emotional instability in the target, rendering them vulnerable to manipulation. During the vulnerable phase, the seducer can associate the target's experience of pleasure with himself while linking the experience of suffering to something or someone other than himself. Through this action, the seducer can guarantee that the target experiences profound gratification linked to the seducer, who can elicit these emotions at will.

Another nefarious application of NLP in the context of seduction involves the utilization of a technique called pattern disruption. This is the scenario in which the seducer uses Dark NLP techniques to prevent his target from engaging in an undesired action and to diminish her logical reasoning and defensive systems. As an illustration, when the target starts providing logical justifications for why she should not be involved with the seducer, the seducer could divert her attention by asking an unrelated question such as "What is your preferred color?" The seducer intentionally interrupts the target's cognitive processes through this action, undermining their protective mechanisms. This prevents the victim from succumbing to their customary routines.

Erasing Painful Memories

Each of us possesses memories that arise at inopportune moments, causing discomfort and hindering our ability to perform optimally. These things are strongly present in our subconscious due to the intense, unpleasant emotions we associate with them. Implementing the whiteout approach can effectively aid in the cessation of ruminating on certain memories.

Initially, contemplate upon a recollection that elicits a sense of unease within you. It may involve situations that are embarrassing, humiliating, or sad. After forming a distinct mental representation, swiftly increase the intensity of the image, causing it to become completely white.

Subsequently, take a few moments to reflect and divert your attention to a completely unrelated matter. Iterate the procedure rapidly and consecutively for a minimum of six or seven instances, then halt to observe the outcome. Upon recalling the distressing memory, it will either fade completely from your mind or become indistinct and difficult to perceive. Incorporating a sound effect during the whiteout process can be beneficial.

Ensure intervals are inserted between each iteration to prevent your brain from forming a repetitive pattern of the image and the whiteout.

Diminish the influential voice of criticism.

Each of us has an internal monologue. Occasionally, the vocal expression resembles that of an individual who previously engaged in faultfinding, such as a harsh instructor or an excessively censorious guardian. Occasionally, the voice we hear is solely a product of our thoughts, a manifestation of our worries and uncertainties. Regardless of the voice's resemblance, it likely has a significant influence on you and can swiftly undermine your self-assurance.

This critical voice appears to be commendable. Our sense of prudence and reason is formidable. However, in actuality, this small voice causes more damage than benefit. The captain, who is uncertain, leads us away from any potential danger. Occasionally, embracing risks to progress in life and achieve our aspirations is necessary. Hence, heeding this small inner voice can severely hinder our prospects of attaining happiness and achieving achievement.

Furthermore, this voice emanates from an unfavorable perspective characterized by uncertainty about oneself. This vocalization conveys our lack of self-belief. As previously mentioned, your level of self-belief is of utmost significance. By lacking belief in oneself and one's capabilities, one intentionally sabotages oneself and establishes a path toward failure.

Therefore, weakening the influence of that skeptical and cautious inner voice that persists in your mind is advisable. Cease empowering the voice by placing belief in its statements. Even the most pressing concerns are not conducive to your achievement. Discontinue the act of listening to and pursuing the ideas it generates, and instead acknowledge the reality that you might indeed have an opportunity.

When faced with the critical voice in your mind that tells you, "You can't do that" or "That's too difficult for someone like you," visualize the voice speaking comically. One can envision a cartoon voice, for example. This diminishes the gravity of the voice. You can start to regard it with less gravity as a consequence. You may find the voice amusing and the uncertainty it instills within you. You come to see that this voice does not possess any authority over you, and the doubts are not something you truly need to be concerned about.

Positive statements or declarations

Positive affirmations can effectively condition your mind to acknowledge specific truths as actuality. Verbalizing thoughts to oneself enhances the likelihood of internalizing these thoughts within the mind. Verbal affirmations can be utilized to assert and instruct oneself in positive beliefs.

Affirmations can encompass a wide range of statements; however, for them to exert a beneficial influence on you, it is crucial that they are formulated positively. Avoid making self-deprecating statements such as, "I am incredibly unintelligent" or "Why did I subject myself to this situation once more?" These affirmations have a pessimistic tone and perpetuate poor self-perceptions.

Instead, affirm beliefs that align with your desires. Engage in positive self-talk. Express statements such as: "I possess positive qualities and exhibit virtuous behavior." "I have the potential to achieve success." "I will execute this task with precision." By reciting these affirmations, you can gradually embrace them as truth and condition your mind to fully believe in them.

Conquer Opposition

A component within you wants to recover and experience improved well-being. You seek to surmount obstacles in your cognitive processes and detrimental self-perceptions that restrict and impede your achievements. However, inexplicably, another aspect of your being opposes the process of improvement. Presumably, this aspect of your behavior is merely a result of routine. You have become accustomed to experiencing discomfort and have sought solace in its familiarity. Hence, some of your being adheres to the pattern of not experiencing wellness, engaging in negative thinking, and avoiding confrontation with your worries. You exhibit an inherent inclination to reject change, even when that change is necessary for a fulfilling existence.

This resistance can appear as a hindrance to your NLP endeavors. Although you diligently perform the rituals and engage in visualization exercises, an external force appears to supersede their effects. Your mind is opting to return to its familiar patterns of negativity and detrimental thought processes.

Acquire the ability to identify and overcome this opposition. Proceed with the utilization of Natural Language Processing (NLP). Over time, your innate defenses will weaken, and you will acquire fresh, beneficial behaviors. Persevere relentlessly. Exhibit unwavering determination in your pursuit of NLP , encompassing the cultivation of optimistic thoughts. Do not allow any individual negative idea to undermine your well-being. You possess superior qualities and capabilities above what is now being demonstrated. When confronted with negative thoughts, simply disregard them and cultivate optimistic thinking. Do not assume that NLP is ineffective or that you cannot utilize NLP .

The Essentials Of Reading People

We're going to examine the foundations of reading people in this chapter. As a result, we'll discuss language, communication styles, and how you can communicate more than you realize while dealing with others.

For the typical individual, communication is just the sharing of information. This is frequently restricted to using words to convey information from one place to another. In truth, language is the facilitator that lets us speak openly and clearly.

It is true that animals can communicate with one another, but their methods are rudimentary and mostly rely on instinctual responses. To defend itself, a dog might, for example, snarl and display its teeth at another.

From then on, we as humans have advanced significantly. Evolution means we can express our true feelings without relying on automatic responses. Our ability to use language to express ourselves clearly to others is a product of our evolutionary process.

This has produced incredible literary achievements. The great literary works of writers like Shakespeare, Dickens, Hemingway, and Miller prove this.

These all illustrate how language has become increasingly important in interpersonal communication due to human evolution. However, it is nearly impossible for humans to interact with one another solely through language due to the vast number of languages that exist.

Take a moment to consider that.

About 300 million of the eight billion people are native English speakers. Furthermore, even though there are roughly 3 billion English-speaking people on the planet, they still make up less than half of everyone on it.

With fewer than a billion native speakers, Hindi is the language spoken by most people worldwide. Not nearly an eighth of the world's population is represented by that. This suggests that billions of people have different linguistic backgrounds.

This is the reason why cross-cultural communication might be challenging at times. Language, or the absence of it, tends to be a barrier for humans. Moreover, when we don't understand what others are saying, we are wired to lockdown. This concept will resonate with you if you have ever been in a circumstance where you were forced to listen in on a conversation in a language you did not understand.

However, language barriers do not prevent human communication. Humans possess an innate communication mechanism that can quickly take precedence over words. "non-verbal communication" is frequently used to describe this kind of communication. All the facial expressions, gestures, and other physical manifestations used to transmit meaning when interacting with one another are collectively referred to as non-verbal communication.

Consequently, nonverbal communication is distinct from verbal communication of any kind. Many gestures and expressions are widely understood and accepted because nonverbal communication is so potent. For instance, almost every culture views a hug as a show of affection. Even though there are customs that dictate when a hug is allowed, hugging is still widely seen as a gesture of affection.

For example, smiles are widely considered a kind gesture worldwide. In most cultures worldwide, yelling is interpreted as an aggressive gesture. As a result, you might not have intended for your tone of voice to convey as much as it does.

The truth is that humans have developed means of communication that enable them to express meaning under critical circumstances. Visual symbology is one instance of this type. Humanitarian workers can be easily recognized during disaster relief operations by the red cross or red crescent displayed on their clothing. This instantly notifies people in the crisis region that these people are available to assist.

Furthermore, a strong message can be conveyed without using language-specific symbols, such as the red triangles that denote danger. Communication is indeed both innate to humans and universal.

Nonverbal communication is employed in daily conversations, yet it's not just for interacting with people from different cultures. Even though they are essential to communication, we rarely give them any thought.

The phrase "it's not what you say, it's how you say it" is one you may have heard someone say.

This phrase essentially captures the essence of nonverbal communication. Nonverbal communication, on the other hand, includes spoken communication, body language, and facial expressions.

This is known as nonverbal communication.

Body language is essential for communicating meaning between individuals. Body language may reveal much about a person, including their thoughts, feelings, and what they truly want you to know.

A typical illustration of this can be seen in the political sphere. Consider the politicians who are seeking reelection. They usually stand up straight and make eye contact with their audience while grinning and using open gestures like spreading their arms.

The candidate's body is sending out these indications immediately. They convey warmth, openness, and assurance. On the other hand, a candidate who displays sagging shoulders, a frown, and crossed arms communicates the exact opposite. They don't give voters a sense of confidence. In actuality, they could give off the impression of unease and distrust.

Politicians must become experts at nonverbal communication to connect with voters and win elections. Stars, religious authorities, and armed forces members are among the others who should become proficient in this art. Military personnel must exercise extreme caution when it comes to their nonverbal cues since even the slightest misstep could be interpreted as an act of aggression and result in a fight that claims lives.

Even while most people do not frequently encounter life-threatening situations (like police and military personnel do), nonverbal communication is nonetheless crucial for success in the commercial sector.

An interview for a job is one significant circumstance where nonverbal communication is crucial. The importance of displaying the appropriate non-verbal clues during an interview is often discussed. The most popular advice is to smile and sit up straight. But there are many more variables at work in an interaction, like a job interview.

Furthermore, a job interview is the greatest illustration of the interaction between verbal and nonverbal communication in a single event. Even if a job applicant says, non-verbal cues will always supersede all the correct things, verbal communication if they indicate otherwise.

www.ingramcontent.com/pod-product-compliance
Lightning Source LLC
Chambersburg PA
CBHW052133110526
44591CB00012B/1705